CW00408727

I Write What I Like

Henderson R Murray

Di
Hope You find A
Poem That resonates
Love
H.   28/11/22

Copyright © 2012 Henderson R Murray
All rights reserved.
ISBN: 1512220833
ISBN-13: 978-1512220834

"DON'T BE AFRAID OF THE SPACE BETWEEN YOUR DREAMS AND REALITY. IF YOU CAN DREAM IT, YOU CAN MAKE IT SO"

- BELVA DAVIS

CONTENTS

- The Cat is Still a Cat
- I Am the Nightmare
- The Void behind His Eyes
- If Only It Was You
- All That's Jazz
- Barbados
- Hidden in a Smile
- Alone with his dreams
- *~ion*
- Remember to Remember
- Saving Faces
- One Word
- Dreadlocks not *shitlocks*
- The Gathering of Like Minded Souls
- A Love That Was Meant to Be
- Cold Blood
- Sheer Pleasure
- Oh Really!
- Normal
- Blackflower
- Who Am I

Preamble

I Write What I Like was in me from small. I love to chat, I love to listen, I love to observe life, drift off in to that parallel space, [those that know me well, call it H world], share my positive, optimistic and enthusiastic thoughts and occasionally vent…that's this book. What you are reading, or about to read…

Poetry (from the Greek poiesis — meaning a "making", more narrowly, the making of poetry) is a form of literary art which uses aesthetic and rhythmic qualities of language—such as phonaesthetics, sound symbolism, and metre—to evoke meanings in addition to, or in place of, the prosaic ostensible meaning. – Wikipedia

If you class my musings as poetry cool, if you don't cool…I am not professing to be a poet, however, my words have been accepted as such by some. I'm fortunate to have been able to stage and attend events, where amazing wordsmiths have been present. Life can be this simple and inspiring. Things I had known, or thought, but never had the words to express, others were capturing in a word, line or verse. I wanted to have a go, I needed to have a go…

From my thoughts came **Soundwaves**, a night of self-expression held in the basement of a nightclub every Tuesday in Dalston. As I write this I stop and smile, frequently…we had nights where there may have been 6/7 people in and 4/5 were part of my team staging the night…then there were nights, standing room only BUT irrespective there was always words shared, inspiration gleaned, gems unearthed. And so I carried on providing platforms for self-expression:-

the expression of one's own personality: assertion of one's individual traits, the expression of one's feelings, thoughts, or ideas, esp. in writing, art, music, or dance. - **www.merriam-webster.com**

See for me, from small, it has always been about self-expression. Now, whether that has been through art, dance, music or writing, it has always been about me expressing my ideas & thoughts and encouraging others to do the same or linking with others who are like minded.

So this book is for those who just wanna **Write What *they* Like! Peace.**

The Cat is Still a Cat

From Guinea Coast to Portugal
It started in 1441
Prince Henry the navigator and 10 Africans
They discovered the New World
The dye was cast
Twenty negars sold in 1619
From Africa to the Americas
The Africans let history tell its own story
The cat is still a cat

Five hundred years
From Africa to the Americas
From the Americas to Europe
An ancient harvest on the Nile
A comfortable house in the suburbs
All can see the way forward
But maybe none can face to look back
You can take a cat to a monastery
But a cat is still a cat

I am the nightmare

I am the nightmare
Hidden deep in the minds of society
I am the monster
To your Frankenstein
I am your worst fear
And it is through your greed
That guess what?
I am here

You lock your doors
And make your laws
With police for keys
And lies as pens
It still hasn't dawned
Even though you were warned
This nightmare never ends

You can't steal a nation
For economic salvation
Without the chickens coming home to roost
Now that we're here
And you're steeped in fear
Guess what?
Your monsters on the loose

Like Nostradamus & seers before
I am blessed
With sight beyond sight
Heed my warning society
Change your ways
Or
Be prepared

For the original fight or flight
The time is nigh
The signs abound
Now with numbers
We are your worst fear
Like the adage says
If you don't hear
You will feel
From me
From us
The nightmare

*[I recited this backed by Max Roach – Garvey's Ghost…it dropped sweet]

The Void behind His Eyes*

Lost and abandoned
He roams the streets
No direction
Aimlessly, walking
Dare you catch his gaze?
For as sure as night follows day
You would see the void behind his eyes

In the birth of a child
They say there is hope
This soulless shell
Was once a child
The systematic rape of hope
Faith
And honesty

Where once dreams and aspirations grew
In fertile soil
There now lies a barren wasteland
With only confusion and anger as scenery
We killed this plentiful crop
For we are society
By accepting that once down
You're down
We poisoned the fertile soil
A tree cannot grow
Without roots
So says the void behind his eyes

Invisible men and women
Walking amongst us
Occupying the street corners
Running the streets
Trying to survive
Raped externally
Scarred internally
Forgotten possibly

Dependent on a system
That doesn't care
Or handouts
From strangers who don't see him
If you catch his gaze
Fill the void behind his eyes
With a smile
Acknowledgement
Of his existence

*[I first performed this in '98 to Miles Davis — All Blues]

If Only It Was You*

today I opened my eyes and was greeted by the sun
if only it was you
as I drew back the curtains
and cracked open the window
the crisp morning air planted a kiss on my cheek
the birds sung with wanton abandonment
their song filled me with the joy of love
i tried to retain every harmonious note
so that I could use it as inspiration
to let you know how much I love you
but I am no bird
and I don't have you
if only love was as easy as waking up
if only you were here
to see how I can be
when I wake
the birds have stopped singing
the crisp air is now muggy
the sun has hidden behind a cloud
as I do when I see you
i close my eyes
and every day is you

*[Robert Glasper Experiment – Calls {Instrumental} goes perfectly
as a backing to this poem]

*All That's Jazz**

When did I develop my love of jazz
I honestly couldn't say
Maybe it was whilst watching Charlie Brown
I can remember Joe cool and Woodstock dropping steps...yeah
But what about that episode of 'I Spy'
Bill Cosby and Robert Culp in the seedy jazz place
Low ceiling,
Smoke,
Goatees,
Rollnecks,
Jazz trio
And everyone's cooooooooool!!!
Nope!
It was on hearing about these vibrant characters
Coltrane, Davis, Monk, Gordon and Parker
Their music was foreign to me
But I remember wanting to become a native
Today we have Pine, Marsalis, Incognito, Acid Jazz and Jazz Fm
Joe cool's on satellite
And the goatee and rollneck have gone
When did I develop my love of jazz
It's not really important
But now I'm a native and it's all cooooooooool!!!

*[Drop this with Miles Davis – Flamenco Sketches and let the jazz n lyrics move you]

Barbados

Barbados animates my skin
It runs through my veins
It seems to help guide me
Along the road of discovery
Along the road
That will help me to understand
Who
I am
And where
I'm
From
However
Barbados it appears
Doesn't know me
And maybe I don't know Barbados
I open my mouth
And I'm called a Bajan
Yet Bajans call me English
And wish my voice to be no more
A mass of water older than you and I
Lumps of land
Within whose shores secrets are buried
Try to distance us
I dream of being one with you
The womb of my parents
And with hope growing ever larger in my heart
The road I journey I know will one day come to an end
And when I look back
It will be with the knowledge that having completed my journey
I have passed Barbados
In to the thoughts of those I Love

[Inspirational when recited to Astral Travelling by Pharoah Sanders]

Hidden in a Smile*

Does my smile warm you?
Does it make you smile – then feel happy?
Does my smile warm you?
When you feel alone, unloved or snappy

Does my smile warm you?
Like the sexual warmth, of a slow, passionate, kiss
Does my smile warm you?
Like the rice 'n' peas on a Sunday, you know you'd never miss

Does my smile warm you?
Jus' me, my teet, an' a grin
Does my smile warm you?
'n' leave you primed for what may or may not begin

Does my smile warm you?
Think hard, think long, think sure
Does my smile warm you?
Knock! Knock! Smile, guess who's at your door

Now it's time for happy – SMILE
Mmmmm...smell the rice 'n' peas – SMILE
Read my mind – SMILE
And as for that slow, passionate kiss – SMILE!

*[This is sweet served with Miles Davis – Blue in Green]

Alone with his dreams*

Let me sleep
Please!
Let me close my eyes
I can hear the music
It's nearing
I pierce the cotton wool clouds
Like a bird I swoop
I can hear the music
It's our music
It's nearing
Ah! The lights...
Those wondrous, mysterious lights
I wonder what she'll be wearing
Blue
No yellow
Or maybe, my favourite green
I wonder what she'll be wearing
I must go faster
Faster
Faster
I must go faster
Or she'll be gone
I see her
She's there
She's waiting
...like she promised
Those cotton wool clouds
She's gone
No she can't have
Where's the music?
What happened to our music?
My lights
Our lights

Our music
I can't see her
It's all dark

No
Not again
Please God! Not again
Let me sleep
Please let me close my eyes

*[Great accompanied by Alice Coltrane – Journey in Satchidananda]

~*ion*

Who should you fear?
The master
The mistress
The bigot or **~*ion***

Who do you fear?
Who? What? Or Where? Is **~*ion***
You know it! But you don't appreciate its' power
In opera*tion* its func*tion* is to maintain its applica*tion*

~*ion* how do you control us?
Oppress*ion*, through this you tried to leave us with no expecta*tion*
Your attempted descriptive explana*tion* was coloniza*tion*
You should have used its real name exploita*tion*

True you're not all bad
Though how you tried, remember subordina*tion*, subjuga*tion*
Ah! But we found your Achilles heel...
Who did you fear? ...faith, belief, yes salva*tion*

We created you though some abused you
They used to make themselves feel strong
We followed their lead, but now who do you fear?
Libera*tion*, emancipa*tion*, or our forgiveness redemp*tion*

So think on again, when asked who do you fear?
The master
The mistress
The bigot or **~*ion***

Remember to Remember
[a poem to be shared and performed with your people –
enjoy!]

You can't get here standing there
Remember to Remember

Each second is growth, therefore change – you can't add to it
or take from it
Remember to Remember

Each tentative step is a starting point
Remember to Remember

It is very simple to make things very difficult
Remember to Remember

Laughter is contagious and what a beautiful thing to catch
Remember to Remember

In the land of the blind, the one eyed man is king
Remember to Remember

Truth kept to oneself becomes a lie
Remember to Remember

You can't clap with one hand, we need to work together
Remember to Remember

Pain is the mother of change
Remember to Remember

This poem's done…what are you gonna do?
Remember to Remember

Peace!

Saving Faces

A sense of human individuality
Personal artistic aims
Tempered by my anxiety
Consciously insulated and protected from views
Exaggerated, manipulated and deliberately denigrated
Here is today's news

A world at war
Changing global and domestic appearances
A world in fear
Where shadows live, breed with no interferences
A world of hate
Where differences are highlighted and similarities are hindrances

But here's the good news
Today you're here, and the bad news finishes
A space for love
Where the like minded share
And negativity diminishes

No room for fear
As collectively we look for local initiatives
No longer are we primitives
We're changing spaces
We're saving faces – just saving faces

ONE WORD

It can take one to start a war **HATE**
It can take one word to end a dream **FAIL**
It can take one word to break a spirit **FOOL**
It can take one word to hold you down **OPPRESS**

BUT

It can also take one word to wipe these all out

YOU DECIDE YOUR WORD

YOU
US
FAITH

Dreadlocks not shitlocks
Could it be
That only I can see
Those brothers
Would be lovers
Who would attempt to turn
Beautiful strong sistas
Into pseudo-surrogate mothers
Claiming to run tings
Tings - Nuh run we
Cos me 'ave de lyrics
de looks
And a big dick
So's me get plenty ah pussy
Are the same brothers
Would be lovers
Who have no respect for themselves
Or their queens...
Are the same brothers
Would be lovers
Who are seldom seen
On the scene
As pride and respect
Manifested itself
As the queen
Who they mis-treated
Dis-respected
And is now not there
So it's oneself to preen
You gave her shit
And often knocks
But now look at you
I've heard of dreadlocks
But shitlocks
.....ah natty dread ah wha' she want!

The Gathering of Like Minded Souls

Ssssssshhhhhhh!
Allow silence to descend
As time we'll suspend
Bask in the fullness
Of the here and now
The individual paths we have taken
Whilst divided
Have led each of us
To this here
This present
This now
So sssssssssssshhhhhhhhhh!
And I'll begin

You may know me
As H
Henderson
Or maybe Fox
Some would call me
The guy with locks
Though I never met him
Dr Seuss would maybe title me
The Black Fox with Locks
In the Red Devil Socks
...now this is not to be confused with
The Dr Seuss classic 'Fox in Socks'

I'm the Inspirer and Inspired
Admirer and Admired

I'm just a guy who pushes creativity
Jazz and Art in its' totality
The you and me in Hu-Man being
Often seeing
The brightest light
When I'm the wordsmith on the night
Who's ascribable to your delight
Creating
Rhapsodic
Rhythmical
Metrical
Words to recite
Often up in the dead of night
Eyes
Mind
And soul
Open for inspiration
Soul
Mind
And eyes open to temptation
Me!
A spoken word artist
Wrong!
I'm just a guy who's a wordsmith pugilist
Loving the flow
Just give
Then I go
Catching the audience
With sideways glances
Standing here
Dismissing
The falsehood
Of

Black men not making advances
Inclusion
Not exclusion
Is my poetic opus
Instead of waiting for providence
Bringing together
The me, you, we, us
Thus
Perpetuating the ethos of 'the Lair'
Where beautiful people come to hear
Talented artistes
Who come to share
A guy with a vision draws you near
Where individual paths
Lead to this Now
This present
This here
What way – my goal
Just this...

The Gathering of Like Minded Souls

A Love That Was Meant to Be

We spoke, but never realised
In time we would play the hands of destiny
A group, a friend an event that was not
Would bring us together – **A Love That Was Meant to Be**

Your image was in my mind from birth
Your love was the chorus to the beat of my heart
A simple glance confirmed, what destiny knew
Through our hearts we would never be apart

To say I believe in miracles, once I could not
Yet since meeting you, I would shout it aloud
My whole being is yours – I Love You! With all that I am
With Gods will and blessing, when you say I Do!

The song plays it's our anniversary today girl
But it forgot the words – it has been ever since I met you
Everyday – good and bad, through the rough and smooth
It will always be us two

You have been a friend, a lover and sometimes a pain
But nothing would I change – I love what I see
I fell in love with you from the first
Thank you with all my heart – for **A Love That Was Meant to Be**

- dedicated to my beautiful Wife C x

Cold Blood

We all read the stories
The voice of the gun speaking loud
The young graves
Now reverberate their decree
Hoping
That you and me
Will see
The futility
In this brutality
If only walls could talk
Under the promise of amnesty
They would tell the truth
Of how society
Has created a new pastime
In keeping with its hunger
For reality tv
The walls say
Nobody knows but me
Of how many more
Young souls
Struck down in their prime
Are asked to form
An orderly line
To ensure the bullet is never hungry
After all
We're not animals
Black on Black violence
Reminiscent of cannibals
Just to retrace history
But His-Story

Is cut short of glory
With mothers screams
Drowning out their dreams
The walls say
They've seen too many die
The gun now a dress accessory
Police wanting to arrest me
For a being a strong Black Man
Whose gun is his mind
And bullet is his knowledge
The walls testify
Of another young man sentenced to die
So as Black, White and Asian mothers' cry
Ask yourself why

Perennially we plant this strange seed
Hoping it'll harvest a new crop
And we can impress Mother Nature
Our creator
With our ingenuity
Thus saying we are not guilty
Of stealing her stock
But we constantly refill her plot
With this strange seed
And new crop
Black meat
For the hungry gun to eat
Can you hear the wall speak

SHEER PLEASURE

in between the sweetness of the kiss
if you can get your woman
to indulge in this
yours will be the richest treasure
as she invites you
into her world
of...**sheer pleasure**
you see
from a young age
it was hard to gauge
when
or where
lingerie replaced
the comfy
reliable
undeniable
underwear
linge
the French for linen
in my thoughts is a given
never forbidden
often ridden
when passion becomes rhythm
far detached from linen
or fabrics of that ilk
damn straight
it's ahl about the silk
or the silk substitute
got's to be
something that shimmies
making you reach for your jimmies
while she's there
looking soft and slick to the touch
not forgetting the lace
incorporated
to make your heart race
as your rhythmic passion – continues at pace

as you uncover the layers
that lead to that precious treasure
let's not forget
how you got there!
through her...**sheer pleasure**
Switch It!
let's work this through
see if you love and cherish your woman
she should
in return
love and cherish you
for though aesthetically
you may not care
if it's silk...lace...or satin!
you should always be aware
that it's something – she feels like a woman in!
you see first off
if you're not reliable
why's she gonna go make herself desirable
lingerie is something she doesn't usually wear
result: you're seduced...
HELL YEAH!
before the seduction has even begun
the mirror tells her she's sexy
the air carries whispers of allure
leading to cries of *More! More!...Encore!!!*
yep! endless fun
now the seduction has begun
so remember that silk...
that feels so good against the skin of the woman
who's wearing it in leisure
in between the sweetness of the kiss
could be your richest treasure
as she indulges you
in her world
of...**SHEER PLEASURE!**

Oh Really!

Now
When I hear IC3
Whether it be
Over the radio frequency
Or
As is so often the case
Blasèly
Worked into my tv
I have to chuckle to myself
As I know
The powers that be
Using the term
IC3
Cannot seriously
Have the temerity
To classify me
With no knowledge or respect
For my history
As the man
Who in all probability
Is the same man
Committing said street robbery
Bald, 5'3
Mmmmmmm sounds like me
Stocky build,
Mousey hair,
Blue eyes
OK guv' it's a fair cop
You got me...
IC3...***Oh REALLY!***

NORMAL

I am normal man
Living a normal life
With normal aspirations and dreams
So say you
I am the fruit of the oldest tree on this planet
Through the years you have tried to cull its' growth
But to no avail
The roots sink deep into the core of all existence
The branches stretch further than the mind's eye
The leaves touch all who come into contact with her
I am the product of Mother Nature
A result of God's love
Descendant of Kings and Queens
Warriors who are yet to be conquered, indomitable
Each day I strive to be better, stronger and more
knowledgeable
My dreams and aspirations know no ceiling
I am a normal man
Living a normal life
With normal dreams and aspirations
So say you
But,
I do it extraordinarily
So say me

Blackflower

The early February chill
In the wee AM's
Has minds wandering
To distant shores
With heart and soul
Packed into your suitcase
As T&T beckons
No more kisses
That last lingering kiss
My mind traces your nakedness
Under those layers
Purveyors
Of amour
Recall thoughts
And bring forth memories
Of their own carnival
The February AM chill
Reminding me
Last call for all lovers
Say au revoir
And remember
Time flies
The wind is me
Carrying you safely to distant Caribbean shores
The breeze on your neck, when you land
Are my kisses
Providing you with protection
From the Caribbean heat
See that's me to
The heat of my passion for you coupled with my smile
Bask in it
For the Caribbean showers
Will keep you cool
As they too are me
Providing the essential water

To allow you to grow
Nurturing all that is you
Grow my Blackflower
Our spiritual soil
We carry with us
Everywhere we go
So we can grow
Independently
And Interdependently
My Blackflower
I am Air! Breeze! Sun & Rain!
I am the gardener
To my Blackflower
I am **Love**

Who Am I?

Who am I
I am the dreamer and the dream
I am the source
A journey towards discovery
For within me lies
In a state of readiness
Embryonic ideas and thoughts
Lifes' rich tapestry
Of in betweens and endings
Divorced by their life partner
Time
Do you just look at me
Or do you actually see me
Who am I
I am the one who escapes mediocrity
I have evaded the expected norm
I see whilst others look
Observing the seconds
That turn past into present
And guide present into future
Bringing into existence ideas & thoughts
Lifes' rich tapestry of in betweens and endings
Divorced by their life partner
Time
I am the dreamer and the dream
I am the source
I am ME

A WORD OF THANKS

Quite a few people have helped, bring this book to daylight. So as night follows day here are a few… with Thanks from me2you…

My amazing wife Claudette aka C: You backed; supported; encouraged; grounded and acted as the occasional muse & audience for me. You gave me space when I went into H being moody/creative mode, and wanted to be alone with my thoughts. However, you also ensured I rejoined the rest of the world regularly. *Love you totally...*

My family: My very special mum/dad & sister, who were there when I held my first event involving poetry 1992. I got my way with words from my dad (Siirrrrrr!) and my way with people from my beautiful mum…and I say what personality plus looked like from the best sister & friend a guy called H could ask for.

Special mentions go out to: My soul sister Bernie [You always got me…Gemini]! Sheromie [You shine brighter than most stars]; My bro Os.G [You were there from Visions]; Eddie @ Visions [the birth place of my poetry – Soundwaves]; Mums – Thanks for Stone Mountain, Atlanta G.A or maybe the book doesn't happen…My gorgeous nieces Paige & Alexander – got bare chat like our families – so here's to the next generation.

My go to girls Pauline & Nikki Dady: your advice and support with turning my thoughts into this book [priceless].

Penultimately - my ace in the hole – my soul coach Melina, 5' and change of Italian not to be messed with, opened my soul to the world of possibility…opened my mind to my innate ability. Love Ya!

Thanks to all the amazing poets/wordsmiths who have crossed my path and inspired me – too many to name, however I wanna call out these cats:-

Shereen the Poet – because you're a WOMAN!
Urban Poet – Ms Harper YOU AIN'T EASY! LOL
Lexi – still remembering the effect of *Chocolate Milk*
Eli Anderson – the original storyteller
Natty – will never forget T5 - you plucked rhymes from air… & left my students in awe!

My torchbearers:
Maya Angelou; Langston Hughes; Imamu Amiri Baraka; Benjamin Zephaniah; John Agard; Oscar Wilde

Humble thanks to the most high – I understand the universe has a time and purpose for everything.

Peace
Henderson
aka Fox
aka H

Printed in Great Britain
by Amazon

75386548R00031